"I love you. Not like they told you love is, and I didn't know this either, but love don't make things nice, it ruins everything. It breaks your heart. It makes things a mess. We aren't here to make things perfect. The snowflakes are perfect. The stars are perfect. Not us. Not us! We are here to ruin ourselves and to break our hearts and love the wrong people and die. The storybooks are bullshit."

—Ronny, *Moonstruck*

Aortic Chaos:

Sorrows of the Hopeless Romantic

ISBN-13: 978-0-692-07848-8

Poetry by: M.N. Bonds
Illustrations: Azure Prince Inc
Cover Design: Tamara Viskovic
Editor: JoyMemo Editions

For other permissions or any inquiries please contact: mnbondswrites@gmail.com

Aortic Chaos:
Sorrows of the Hopeless Romantic

M.N. Bonds

Illustrated by Azure Prince Inc

Acknowledgements

I would like to dedicate this book to all the brave lovers, friends and family who supported this creation, my daughter whom inspires me to be bold, carefree, and confident to share my heart and passion. Moreover, none of this would be possible without the men who broke my heart whom I should have bitter reserve for, but prison is not for me. I still believe in love after the storms and you should too...

Chambers of Contents

Part I: *We Have a Situation*..............**1**

   1. Petals 3
   2. Short Hand............................ 4
   3. Chaos.................................... 6
   4. Treasure Hunt 8
   5. Nowhere 15
   6. Illusion................................. 17
   7. Realize.................................. 20
   8. Second Chance...................... 23
   9. Protocol 24
   10. Smash................................. 26
   11. Enough 29
   12. I Tried 31
   13. Distressed Fire 36

Part II: *Rise of the Insecurities*..........**41**

   14. Reflection 43
   15. Worthless 44
   16. Turnoff 45
   17. If Only 47
   18. Malfunction.........................49
   19. Chase..................................50
   20. You Can't Blame Her
       (Monologue) 51
   21. Easy Street........................... 56

Part III: *Reflections of a Broken Heart* **59**

22. Remorse 61
23. Demolition............................ 64
24. Totaled 66
25. Technical Difficulties 68
26. Nerve.................................... 72
27. Wound 74
28. Toxic Love 76
29. Never Again 78
30. Too Late 80
31. Miss Faithful 82
32. I Win 87
33. Heart Attack......................... 88
34. Genuine 94
35. Finale 96

Part I

We Have a Situation

"I wish I knew how to quit you."

—Jack Twist, *Brokeback Mountain*

Petals

He loves me
He loves me not
Sometimes I feel we are lovers
Sometimes I feel we are friends
Now suddenly, nothing
I forgot I'm your benefit
And you mine too, totally unfit
The difference is
That I'm not using you

Short Hand

I thought it was something special
But the value is steadily fading
Because the move to make me yours
For it, I'm still waiting for the anointed
hours
And I don't know how long I can hold
out
This patience is burning out
It shouldn't take this long to think
And it's killing me, am on the brink
Because every day the deeper in love I
sink
And I need to know, honestly
Am I wasting my time?
To you, this may be cool
Okay, fine
But I have to draw the line

I think about you each day
I think to tell you these thoughts
But the words never leave my mouth
No matter how I converse, no matter
how deafening
They stay trapped in the chambers of
my heart
Because I never know where to start
And I wonder every second of the day
If you're thinking of me in the same
way
Or am I alone?
Being a fool on my own
Telepathically I wish we could sync

But part of me is scared
Scared for what you might think
And the other part wants to know
Decipher every crevice, wrinkle of your brain
And not having clarity is driving me insane
Causing me much suffering and pain
I wish you could see all that you've got
Do you want this or not?

Maybe you do, maybe you don't
Don't waste my time
I can procrastinate on my own
Either love me or leave me alone

TYPING . ..

Chaos

What hurts the most
Is that love seems lost
It hurts that the one you hold so close
Is also the furthest away
Close in a physical distance
But emotions miles apart
Shadows mask their heart
A wandering soul, feeling like a clone
And you can't help but feel alone
And for them, you have this love
But of it, you do not say
Because you cannot feel their spiritual
pulse
If they feel the same way
Even when they say they do
It's hard to know if it is true
Because you feel so far apart
Lost, and the connection no longer
exists
And you ask yourself
How am I supposed to feel?
When emotions exist
In a condition such as this
Loving confused
Loving in mystery

Treasure Hunt

You are here
But to find you I need a map
And you claim that you know me
Yet you cannot see I am hurting
I thought that I knew you
But it feels we are drifting apart
And that is what brings us here
As I'm seeking knowledge for both of us
What are we? Who are we?

What do we have to cherish?
Beyond this physical, we have perished
I'm after truth and sincerity
I try to show you how to keep me till
eternity
But it's like you are not hearing me
Trying to teach you in all your
complications and difficulties
Challenging
Drowning in your shallow waters

Gasping
Becoming a victim of your demons
I am in a tight position
Where I am only capable of doing so
much
When I call for you, when I need your
touch
The communication is nonexistent
And for you to beckon me is a rarity
The way I chase you is becoming
embarrassing

Why that is so, I am digging to find
clarity
Loving you is dangerous

Yet you deceive me real good
Makes me a real fool
Convince me
As to why I shouldn't consider myself a
stranger
That I mean more
The world to you

But to show you I never really had the
chance
Your lack of interest often shut me
down
Now I'm standing on this ground
Lost
About you
About us
Our nonexistence
Myth
Or whatever you want to now call this
If we communicated, about all these
I believe we would be able to decipher
the map
And move along the dotted lines to the
treasure
Beyond just another X
And find each other's souls and spirit
And love you would not fear it
Discover personalities

Discover exactly who we both are
But the hands of time do not wait
And the numbers read late
Trying to move forward, to find our fate
For some time I have been willing to go
But fact is you are stubbornly refusing
to move
To open your eyes, to love

Better yet
They are open wide shut
I just don't know; I am crying
I feel like giving up,
Why do I keep trying?
Maybe it will take another type?
A woman who is not me, someone to
fight

Because I can't seem to make you happy
As we are not fine, far from right
Darkness far from light
Is it really worth it, being this sad?
Growing my emotions into deeper frustrations
Constantly reminding me makes me feel bad
Reminding me how you cannot stand me
Or being told reality, that we cannot be
And when I show you the mirror
It cracks on you, nothing binds
As you stand blind
And I rush to mend the now disheveled pieces
And I blame myself for everything
Just so we can get past, and make peace
And we end up in hell all over again
When we don't have to be
A cycle that gets old
As I provide the simple solution, that's bold
But it seems too hard for you to grasp
In this condition, we will never last

I look to them, him to get what I'm missing
Silently wishing I was looking to you
Hoping that you would be my everything
How do you expect me to prove?

When every time I come to win you I
lose?
Every day for you, in and out, I feel like
a fool
Because of you
Fear instills itself back into my bones
of love
As I try to make something, nothing
prospers
That I am learning never really was,
I am left to ponder

I let down my walls at one point
And then the next moment
I was hit with a just kidding
Can you blame me?
Do you have any reason?
As to why you're so difficult?
Are you afraid to say?
Shady for no reason
Not a good play
I can want this
But it soon becomes vain, no way
And means absolutely nothing if you
don't too
Tell me the truth, don't hurt me
I would do the same for you

But I am just another piece
One of your countless women, one of
your prey
To be treated like a lady
I am not worth it apparently,
I feel betrayed

I say this all to you, as I sit in my room
Afar from a distance, the atmosphere is
gloom
Equivalent to the one you put me in
Pouring out my thoughts on you
Wishing you were here to understand
To talk, to share, to help me stand
But that is an unfortunate fantasy
As I wonder why I try, it remains a
misery
Why I give my time
Still, I am staring into the distance
Trying to find you
Trying to find the truth

Nowhere

I turned them all down for the hope of
you
But you failed me and never came
through
I guess I made us more than we were
I guess I was just an intermission
I mistakenly inferred
Different
A bridge for you to stand on
Safe and dry from lonely waters
Then when you crossed to her side
With a knife, you cut my corners
I hate that I felt like a season tide
To you, just a phase
I really thought from heartbreak
You were going to save the day
But instead, you left me in a cold
winter
Anguished and astray
And in a race, I thought I was winning
You had already finished
At the starting line
A year ago
It started back there fine
I thought we were truly going to be
something
But instead it went nowhere, we are
nothing
Hoping you to want to be my everything
And now in my life, you have become
deduced
Empty and nothing

What I thought was never really was
But an illusion

Per Usual

Am I the only one who ended up in
love?
And, like a fool, took things to heart?
Learning that your words were silly
nothings
Poisoned from the start
Just a good flirt to get you through the
day
Until what you desired came into play
Making it safe for your eyes
To finally throw me aside
Failing to acknowledge my feelings
inside
Initiating operation hyper-lie
Here I was offering the benefit of the
doubt
I am asking myself why
Making excuses for you, digging you
out
Thinking that maybe you felt used
Or that I was making the same "single"
moves
But really
The honest truth
Is that I was waiting on you

Illusion

Silly for me to believe
To honestly think that you'd want me
Silly of me to think that I'd ever have a
chance
Chance of being your lady
At one point
I truly thought I did
But once again I overbid
And overestimated
Myself
I have a lot to offer besides beauty
But you wouldn't know
Of my intellectual acuity
Because you don't appear interested
Disregarding my internal, I can attest

The place where you would see truth
That I am so much more, better than
the rest
And be blown away by my heaven for
you

How much I care
The way you make me smile
How often you make my day
The way I feel when you're not here
Words cannot be enough to say
How my nights are sad

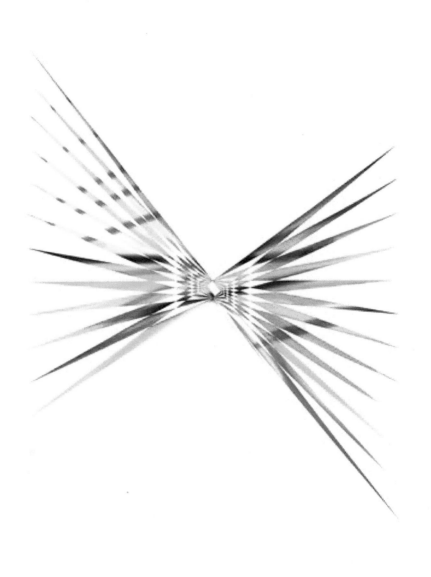

The way we kiss
The way you smell
How you sleep in bliss
How this all goes beyond your sexual
appeal
And to be with me feels real

To think you would want me
As your everything
The truth in which I've never had
So I think hard
The best man that I have truly ever
known
And it breaks my heart, I frown
To know that I can't have you
Because you just want us to be friends

And to me, ours is more than benefits,
And to them, how come you can't resist
Especially when their bad treatment
persist
And to see you the same is what makes
it hard
Especially when I love you
Where it leaves me confused
Because it seemed like we were tightly
fused
And now we are here somehow
Me and you
In your illusion

Realize

In public, you act like you're my man
We stay close; we hold hands
But when we are alone or apart
Somehow the
differences start
We become, torn apart
Wait for it,
Just Friends

I can't understand
It is to my mind rather
confusing
I can't stand it
Are you scared?
Do you like me?
Is my whole company
just amusing?
It is torture to sit and
think in these
moments
Wanting your heart
But deeply wondering if I will ever own
it
It was yours from the start

The things that we do
I do with no one else
And you say that you do with no one
else
So why do we continue to lie to
ourselves?
What are we waiting on?

Right in front of each other
Any day we could be gone
And if one of us be left, when we drift
further
Face the regret of what wasn't said
And only capable of wandering in
mystery
Where if we took a chance

Where love maybe could have led
But for now, wait for it
We just friends

You can put me in a cage
Bookmark me like a page
In your mind for your convenience
Put thoughts of me away
Provoke your conscience
Really is it okay, or will we pay?
And you can pretend that at times I
don't exist
But listen carefully, know this
You can act like you don't care
But in the end, I will be here
But not in the box and places
Where you left me, lost without a trace
But gone, and left all alone
Where you might wake up to realize
That you sir, are lonely

Second Chance

After what you put me through
Again I have given into you
Baby, can you think of me enough to
be faithful?
Consider my heart and resist
temptation?
Resist becoming something love would
despise?
And remain honest as my guy?
Can you think of me more than her?
Think of us, don't shy

This I deserve
I shouldn't have to ask
Not to be last
I am the one you love
Right?
I'm abiding by the rules, not a hard
task
And I feel that you should too
Your absence up's my care
Missing you, wish you were here
Worrying about you there
It's hard to fight this fear
The fear of losing you has reappeared

Protocol

Text instead of call
I feel like the effort is just protocol
To get away with not being chewed
For saying nothing at all out of the blue
Good morning
Good night
Vague details in between
But if I call you out
That's a siren for an automatic fallout

But if I ignore you
All of a sudden you want to know
Why I'm trippin
Blow me up
And when enough is enough
I give in; it's been tough
While you go right back
To doing the same things
I just want you to be sincere
About the loose strings

Don't tell me what you believe I want to
hear
I can feel when the energy is real
I can feel the pain in my ears
So I write my Novocain, I need to heal

Smash

You pried me open and told me to
speak my mind
And to hold my thoughts in
Make yesterday the last time
Between the lines of communication,
I would say I'm fine
But I'm not fine
And picked up that all along I had been
lying
To stay strong I had been trying
Because in my brokenness
I was overcome with fear that you
would contribute to building my
weakness
And sink me to that dark place
Deeper
Throwing it back saying its too thick
Keep this
Leaving me speechless while you hold
my secrets
Shattering me into a million pieces
Using me against myself
The shards of me to cut my own soul
Slashing my heart, wasting my love
Littering me instead of upcyling
Leaving me trashed
In this world ass is first
And sadly
Love is last

Enough

I didn't know, but now I do
Now I hate the fact
That I am in love with you
It is not an act
I wish I could stop instantaneously
But unfortunately, it doesn't work that
way
Why me? It happened spontaneously
I thought we had something good
Something that was to stay
But I guess not
Master of your craft
You had me fooled; it was your tact

I wish I could take back every tick of
my time
Rewind and reverse
The thoughts of you, maybe I'd feel fine
A waste of my mind
Because Lord knows
Your ungrateful ass
To my kingdom was underserved
And I am just your lass
And a fool of a queen, for being in my
nerves
I refuse to any longer be her

In my past relationships
I have always ended up being alone
So a real loyalty
I have never known
Because they always ended up

In him not being my own
Apparently, I am not the type worth
fighting for
They always sneak around
Or let me walk out the door
With no rebuttal
Hard to know how it would be without
me
So they find it easy to set me free
After the experience turned brutal
And time elapses, no more plea

I go through episodes of pain and
sadness
Beating myself up, angry, the madness
Until they decide with their downgrade
substitute
They are through
Because their new love fling has faded
And, like an open invitation, with their
shit
Asking, "Where can I put my stuff?"
Not knowing
When they let go, I also closed my
hands
I am not in the market of layaway plans
I am a Goddess
I am showered with their repentance
I forgive, but not forget
Leave my absence as vengeance
Don't get it twisted, Go
I am a rarity, a royalty
I only come around once

I Tried

It's like the more I tried
The more I failed to love you
Stuck in a position, tired
It was never enough
I don't know what else to do
I tried and tried
And every time I put effort in
It was denied
I was left rejected and dejected
All my efforts had been neglected
Like I had accomplished nothing
It was by love that I trusted you
I gave you everything
And of your heart, I would wonder
Will I ever win? Or was it a plunder?
And say to myself
"If I have to try this damn hard then
maybe I shouldn't shouldn't love him.'
Is it really worth it?

And the outside world agreed
But I ignored them; they were real
Why?
Because this was between me and you
My heart felt different, something felt
by few
Because I was reminiscing back to the
times
Times before my suffering
The way you are now is not promising
The person you have become
I don't know where you went

I can't seem to understand, makes no
sense

And I have tried to the best of my
ability
To comprehend in agility
I want it all to make sense again
When you were happy, I was happy
But now we have lost the gains
I have tried to figure it out
Suppressing my voice, threatening to
shout
And reverse the turns
I just refuse to let all that we have burn

When I call
You don't pick up at all
I never intend for an argument
The direction all things suddenly went
You would call me a bitch when I
questioned
Anything about our relationship
You don't mention
Our communication, not worth our
friendship,whatever the hell we call this
Led me to question your dedication
When all I wanted was more than your
time
I wanted actions, your attention
Every day I was feeling less and less
like the
Light of your lime

Being left off of your list
A phone call, text or a kiss
To see you
I should not have to request this

Ones that are not past 12, 1 or 2 am
That shows me how important I am
I am always the one making the
attempt
But now I think I get the hint
You've made me feel exempt

To say what was on my mind
I tried
I tried to inform you how I felt; I felt
blind
But you wouldn't listen
You're selfish as hell!
Not now or then, not even a call at ten
I tried to talk, on deaf ears it fell
And you would just walk
In tears, I would then yell
But still, you were unmoved to care

My love for you was far from an act
This is evidence, as I am trying to save
this fact
I would even go as far as to write you
letters
I have tried everything
In attempt to make us better
I don't know what else to do
Now here I am leaving you
This is my last resort
The final verdict in my hearts court

You had me so close in your arms
I was captivated by all of you, by your
warm
Not alone, your charm
Beyond my physical, we were firm
My soul was so close to reach
How to love me, baby
I tried to teach
And any closer
Figuratively, you'd be on my shoulders

You would have held me inside
But you could not see this
Because too soon you had put me to
the side
I wish you would open your eyes
See what is in front of you
Perhaps you would realize
Who I am

I don't know you anymore
Have I changed? Don't I glow?
Who are we?
As strangers
Is this how we end the show?
It is because of this that we fight
I know you like the moon knows the
night
And I'm beyond frustrated; I'm in pain
As I'm trying for a love that you made
vain
I cannot continue to play this game
Nothing changes, it's all the same

Distressed Fire

Lately, I've had some hard sunrises
I should've known that eventually
I'd fade in your eyes; it wouldn't be a
surprise
That you'd turn away from the bright of
my rays
No matter how beautiful, I'm at bay
No one likes to stare at the sunshine
I was bright and sacred like a shrine
But only because you gave me energy
Every morning, every day, we were a
synergy
And you have now faded
And now so am I, jaded
I don't want to be the moon or a
billionth star
It's just not the same, we are bizarre

I loved you with photosynthesis
You were the seed of my ray's eye
Neighbor to the clouds up above in the
sky
We struggle daily to forget your name
In rainy season, we were a burning
flame
Washing the heart of the earth new
And it does no good because in a few
moments, it quickly dries

Why do I still exist to try?
Oh! How much you gave to this fire in
the sky
I wish you knew
And it's like nothing I can do to subdue
Absolutely nothing to do about it
You're gone
"Should I let bygones be bygones?"
I ask myself

The thought of you providing for a new
heaven
As I sit sadly and darkened inside
Thought your heart was a haven
Memories honk my mind like a
daunting circus
Haunted by this endless cycle
That is heartrending
Sadly

Natural to me, I am strong
It's hard to shine upon a new seed
I thought I'd have you fully in time
At my beck and call, when I'm in need
Fall is when some things fall apart
But we were a different story
What was previously falling, shattered
And from the crash you saved me
Then winter came
My happiness that you rekindled
continued
Then spring
Now summer
Diversely we fade slowly
Patiently for you, I waited
But eventually, the sun must set

The sun can sometimes waste its time,
When its fiery soul is not desired to
shine
Trying to give your heart and soul
Vitamin D
The shades you chose denied it
Wanting to raise our temperatures
I wanted us to go higher, to cool the
pressure
Crying rivers that have left my heart
empty

A love drought
Only in your life for a period, I never
thought
How do I keep shining?

Part II

Rise of the Insecurities

"People call those imperfections, but no, that's the good stuff."

—Sean Maguire, *Good Will Hunting*

Reflection

How did I let this happen?
I let my guard down and look at me
now
How stupid could I be?
Did I really think love was into me?
Love was in me
But to be reciprocated was a fantasy
Maybe it is my fault, I fancied
Was I desperate?
Was I overbearing?
Was I predictable?
What is it?
What did I do?
What is wrong with me?

Worthless

I wasn't worth being faithful
I wasn't worth big or little conversation
I wasn't worth your intimacy
I wasn't worth to be seen in your sight
I wasn't worth support
I wasn't worth being spared the hurt
I wasn't worth the truth
I wasn't worth your heart
I wasn't good enough for you
I was nothing
I was insignificant to you
Thinking I was something

Turnoff

I'm such a turnoff
Faithfulness is a trait most undesirable
I'm such a turnoff
Making the unbearable bearable
I'm such a turnoff
My independence is hated
I'm such a turnoff
Being nice is lame
I'm such a turnoff
Caring will get you nowhere
I'm such a turnoff
Honesty is not cool everywhere
I'm such a turnoff
Writing and speaking sweet words is a
no-no
I'm such a turnoff
Telling him, you miss him
How dumb could I be?

I'm such a turnoff
Beauty doesn't know me
I'm such a turnoff
My happiness and my smile
I need to calm it down as my style
I'm such a turnoff
Waiting patiently
Expecting you, really?
I'm such a turnoff
Buying you things, sorry
I'm such a turnoff
Enough of these worries

Listening to you about anything
Bad move
I'm such a turnoff
Never arguing
I forgot how it was not sexy
I'm such a turnoff
Always forgiving, baby I'm sorry
I'm such a turnoff
Being intelligent, let me dumb it down
I'm such a turnoff
Falling in love with you, a forgotten
story
I should've known you'd run away
I'm such a turnoff

If Only

If only I refused to care
Refused to share
Opted to lie
Never asked why
Put up a fight
Creeped at night
Ignored the calls and the text
Was about nothing more than sex
Refused to try
Never wanted us to fly
Never loved
Never kissed
Never hugged
If a had shrugged
If I only I did those things
I would have a better reason
For why you're leaving
If only

Malfunction

Too kind
Too caring
Too loving
Too patient
Too calm
Too cool
Too weird
Too slow to anger
Too smart
Too creative
Too nice
Too giving
Too happy
Too optimistic
Too real
Too good
Too good to be true

And because of these judgments, they
let me be
Say they can't stand it, and in turn,
they hurt me
How do you stop being?
People say "you're too much."
But you're just being you
It's nothing you can stop
Nothing you can change
Maybe I'm to blame
For all these shames

Chase

I'm the woman
that men don't
chase
I'm not worth it;
I'm a waste
I'm the woman
that men ignore
I feel invisible
more and more
I'm the woman
that people take
advantage of
Because they don't know how to handle
love
And I'm not the type to chase
Only because my time I can't afford to
waste
I need to know that you want me
And seriously
Not my body only to prey
I'm done with those days
Where my genuine love gets played
There's a new set of directions
My heart this time is in total protection

I'm not Hasbro, Chantel or Mattel
A good man I wouldn't have to tell
And to win
He would seek the goddess within

You Can't Blame Her (A Monologue)

You can't blame her...

When she's so used to being put down, rather than lifted up when it's routine to be emotionally chastised for who she is. Accused of assuming she's perfect,because they judge her life to be so. Judge it because she's not going through what they're going through, but yet she's trying to. For every attempt that she tries, she's pushed away and then ridiculed for not being there when they needed her most. Even though she knows that's not the case, she still becomes slashed. She can't help how God made her, how He blessed and internally dressed her. However, she doesn't flaunt it; she doesn't boast. But his jealously misses seeing her worth and her beauty, her normality. He misses seeing her trying to care, trying to love him, her sweetness and kindness to him, giving her all. But he doesn't miss the opportunity to tell her how he hates when she's happy, that she's too smart for her own benefit, that she's too thriving and feels that she'll outdo him in life, how her vocabulary intimidates him, and a host of negatives. Oh, the things he would say! Idiot! Above his insecurity she continues to try, as it weakens her-weakens her until she starts to feel insecure too, worthless, and wrong. She is far from being at fault for anything, but he doesn't know her past. He doesn't know her battles, her struggles or adversities, and was never willing until it was convenient for him. That time never came, as he would say they had all the time in the world to build and know each other. But how can you build when he's making it a point to shut her down, because his world, is in destruction? You can't blame her when she cries or doesn't believe you when you claim to see what they couldn't. You can't blame her when she's scared and holds back all of who she is because she thinks you'll hate her.

You can't blame her...

When she's so used to being a victim of the unfaithful-never having a man of her own. She makes them priority, as she is loyal and faithful to whom she has committed. Yet, only comes to find in every cycle that she had become an option-an option because they took her kindness for weakness, labeling her naïve.

She was everything- smart, caring, respectable, easy going, slow to anger, funny, giving, unconditional, what a real man would have seen as desirable. So they run with it thinking that she'd never find out, but God will always reveal the truth to his people and stop evil in its tracks. What you sow is what you reap. Because she planted a good seed and him not, he ends up without her. He traded her for drama and less of everything he had and now wants her back. She ends up without him because God has for her something better. However, these aren't her immediate thoughts. In fact, she feels like a blind fool, and partially like it was her fault. She feels she should have changed when he complained about her being too good of a girl. She feels she should have been less nice, less kind, inflicted arguments and chaos, lied, cheated, and everything that in relationships people consider "normal." And when it's not, and peace is in abundance for some reason it's strange, odd. She feels maybe she shouldn't have been so weird, and maybe played like the bad girls. She feels worthless, like there is nothing good about her. Because despite what she had, she wasn't able to keep him, so she feels inadequate at the moment, and it is her lack of trust. So don't blame her when she's scared and cries because you tell her how much you love and appreciate her when you mean it. You can't blame her when she doesn't believe you at first that of this you only foster for her. You can't blame her if she now has walls.

You can't blame her....

Easy Street

How hard is it to stop lovin?
All you gotta do is stop carin`
Stop thinking
Remembering how it used to be
All you gotta do is, end thinking about
"we"
Get rid of all the special things
Throw away the flowers, teddy bears,
rings, pictures and sentimental pieces
Get rid of everything, that you may
have peace
All you gotta do is find somebody new
Say forget them, forget the tasteless
stew
All you gotta do is stop crying
Get hard, stop whining
Don't let anyone buck at your heart
How hard is it to stop lovin?
And make a fresh new start

All you gotta do is snatch yourself back
Take back your soul
Reclaim your heart; it wasn't your foul
All you gotta do is erase them from
your life
Delete them from your phone
Lose all contact, reflect alone
All you gotta do is say no
Be like an anti-love
Never again say yes

All you gotta do is...
All you gotta do is...
All you gotta do is...

How hard is it to stop lovin?
Somebody answer me please!
Is it that easy?
Or is it that hard?
To cease feeling mad
To recover from a broken heart?

Part III

Reflections of a Broken Heart

"Nobody puts baby in a corner."

—Johnny, *Dirty Dancing*

Remorse

Remember these are the words you said
So do not confuse this with ego or a big head

"You're overpowering me as a man"
"No woman should be smarter than I am"
Feeling dim, but yet I am yours
We have been through this too many times before
Endlessly, you try to shut me down
Knowing good and well that I do not deserve
The way you pull my emotions around
You complain that I never have time for you
I take it into consideration
And some things I cancel or move
And what do you do?
Make plans in place of my plans, our plans, and never show up
Leaving me standing with confused hands
What the fuck?

You don't call me
You don't text me
But you want to hit me up thinking you

can sex me
Wrong.

I call you
You're tired, sick, or blatantly just hang
up
You're such a liar
The truth I know
Just waiting for you to blow
You hate when I am happy
So in misery you try to trap me
These words came from the den of your
lips
I can't believe those condescends I once
kissed

To want your time
You call me needy and out of my mind
To expose my soul
You call me weird as your eyes roll
In and out is how I let you walk
I hate that I love you
I wish we never talked
You were the first in years that I
trusted
And with my decision I'm disgusted
I have no more tolerance for you
Or the shit you put me through

Demolition

That wall
I should have never let it fall
It was too soon
Brick by brick I let you chip
merrily away
To a distant place like the
moon
Clever you
Big bad wolf
But now
Now I need to rebuild and
renovate
I should have looked further
Beyond the peephole
Then maybe I would've known
That in your game, I was a pawn
That you weren't what you claimed
Your identity to be
But my soul is optimistic to clearly see

Gave you the benefit of doubt
And by doing so, I became your slave
Took me for granted, misused me
throughout
You didn't deserve me; I was naive
You just lost a good girl
It is because of people like you
that I built this wall in the first place
And I see it fell prematurely without a
trace

But as I'm writing, the new one is
already done
It didn't take long

And in fact, it's even higher and
stronger
Sometimes we are best fitted and
suited
To care for ourselves
I've learned this by allowing myself to
be hurt for the last time
To fall like a fool to another fool
Who was more foolish between the two?

How blessed he was to know and have
me
But not anymore for us to be
No more being defeated by a wolf
I'm bigger
I'm badder
And he wants to say something
To see me ever again for anything
In the essence of my entirety
He is unauthorized in my sincerity
He can leave a sticky note if he pleases
Let the trees and the bees read it
For all I care, I moved on from his
misses
He can talk to the wall if he deems fit
My hand he has lost
This is how my heart feels
When I called myself loving him

Totaled

We were on this road together
I gave you the wheel
And I gladly rode the passenger
Driving at a steady speed, coasting
Calm
I thought your love would be all I would
need
The car we drove was customized
indeed
Only made for us to drive on
In fact, we designed our own
I couldn't have had this ride of love
alone

Suddenly
You decide to take your eyes off of me
My safety was thrown to the wind
And we began crashing into trees
Then when the rain came down,
We hydroplaned several feet
Crashing into every last thing in the
street
As we swerved in and out through the
lines
As I begged you to pay every attention
Hoping that we would be fine
Before you take my life
Painful like a heart pierced with a
sharp knife
Now broken down
It won't start

Technical Difficulties

I have stories within me, deep inside
Stories I want to tell you and the world
outside
But you won't take the time
To really hear me, baby
You say you do
But really you don't
Know who I really am
To be heard like this in your so called
forever
I refuse
I feel like a stranger
Every time I come near
There is a loss of connection
Even within the affection
I try to talk to you with perfection
But somehow it seems like you really
don't care
As I read from the facial expressions
Your body language shows you are not
here

No real feedback on what it is
to what I have been saying
Showing opposition
Instead of interest and proposition
Am I really that weird?
Why should I continue my sentence?
When you treat my conversation like it's
obscene
We are here, but I feel so far away

Because I don't feel your concern in any way
For what I have to say
Like around you
You can't appreciate me being myself
And who I am
I refuse to put myself up to dust on a shelf
You make me not want to tell you a word
Not another piece of my life or what goes on in it

But you just sit in silence
Being in your presence is purposeless
Because if you don't care
Or can't handle me ,what's on my mind
One or the other, why should I be there?
How can you possibly say that you do for me?
When it is my mind and heart beat
That composes my inner being
Who taught you how to listen?
The only thing you seem to understand is my kisses
But sadly they do not speak even about the issues
Or for what it is that I truly want to give to you

Want you to know, about my inner
goddess
This queen

What if I stopped those?
I wonder what would be left of our
connection
Being that seems to be the only line
you open
Never leave a dial tone to my emotions
The line between you and me
Cannot be drawn with a pen
Can I even say it is existent?
That's what makes us awkward to
some extent
You say you like our differences
But this is not a difference
This is a communication issue, not an
offense
Nothing new
The perfect force to push me away
So do not expect me to hear you
When you ask me to stay

Nerve

Come to find
I was wasting my time
You said we were fine
So no one would find out
About me, and my whereabouts
You must have been cheating
But on her or me is what I can't decide
I'm real with you; my heart can't hide
So why is it so hard for you to do?

You lie to me like it's nothing at all
But in reality, something big is wrong
Knowing this, my heart is an empty
hole
Sometimes, thinking about all these
Kills me deeply inside
They say that the truth hurts,
But suspicions, desire for answers that
never ceases
Feels just as worse, no peace
When the possibility is high
That they're not a lie

You have nerve
My emotions to take advantage of
Having me believe you were enough
Love that to you never truly was
I'm tired of being used like an ass
My character, everything I stand for
Being abused to the fore
And it's far from being okay
It's not and never will be justifiable
In having treated me this way

And you act fine like everything is fit
Like everything is alright
But you'll regret it
As all darkness meets the light
As the Karma Reaper starts its mission
And you feel like something's missing
Then look to see that it is
Hope that you're prepared for this
To find there's no more me
You can no longer pull me along
like a sing-along
I am not karaoke, but the real song
I'm gone

Wound

It's going to take more than a band-aid
A super-deluxe first aid kit
Or a bottle of new skin
Neosporin sprayed
Benzyl ointment
Alcohol wipes
Painkillers
To clean, soothe, and cover the wound
Deep slashes
Left in my love for him
It's bleeding with pain
As he actually never felt the same
Infected with lies
Hovering flies
Burning from the salt of the tears that
clean, yet burn my eyes unable to see
My heart is cut deep inside
I always fall and get scraped
Why?

Why can't I stay out of the street?
And keep to the beat of the sidewalk
And learn to control my feet
On the pedals of my bike
And remember to wear my helmet
To protect my mind
Elbow and kneepads to break my fall
this time
With love, I took a risk, and I ended up
like this
And the only thing to heal, surely no

one's kiss
The only thing to stitch it is time

And hope for everything to turn out
sound
Besides, you know how long that takes
But I will just have to wait,
With this wound in my love, I'm afraid
And he does not care because
In love he never was
False kisses and hugs
But I rather let him go
So I won't be an injured fool anymore

Toxic Love

I'm a hazard to my health
I'm better off by myself in this stealth
Where if I love too much
I can never get enough
I am my own trust
Where I can't be accused
And by no one can I be used
Nor played dumb for a fool
Where being me is just cool
But when will I learn
The world is not like me; it's tall
If it were, things would be more
peaceful
I tend to give my all
Figuratively, this last name
Bonds, for all its fame
I declare it makes me fall
Ironically, it should have made us bond
Rather or not I want to
It's like nothing I can do
It's merged into my personality
And it causes me to be friendly
Sometimes I can't help the heart
The Lord God gave me

I try to love wisely
But instead, I'm too much like his child
Falling for the same steps endlessly
And it hurts me in the end
I'll be the last to do one wrong
It seems like I'm the last to know

What's going on?
Why does it have to be me?
The girl who loves so easily
Love cripples me instead of setting me
free
I'm a hazard to my health
I'm better off by myself in this stealth
Because I know what I am worth
As well as what it is that I deserve
By myself now, no more pain in my
nerves
It's only me who will make it work

Never Again

I told myself that I would never
Ever let myself stand in this place
again
Having to go through the pain
But of course, I lied to myself again
And once again
I let myself be a broken piece of art
A painting left sideways, tipped off the
easel
Desolate like a deserted hut
A portrait crooked, uneasily lifted
As it sways on the wall
A chiseled stone of beauty shifted
Out of place on its stand
Was I meant to be an exhibit of fool
display?

Because that is what I sometimes see
Why does it happen to this girl? To me?
Am I supposed to give my all?
While disregarding its non-
authenticity?
Don't I deserve true love in my lifetime?
If so, God let me know, of sincerity
And if not, love
I'll just leave it and its components
alone
And my heart and soul can dance
together

To a man
I will never ever
Unless I know for sure
Without a shadow
Or mirage of a doubt
I vow, vow, and re-vow for that vow
As I stand here, in this place of
heartbreak
For the last time
Never, ever, ever
Again

Too Late

"Hey Stranger"
Ugh
Here we go again...

You put me down
And look at you now
You were the one who didn't want me
And now all of a sudden
I'm where you want to be
Don't you remember that you threw me
aside?
Now all of a sudden
You're concerned if I'm alive
Saying that you missed me
That you want me to be your wife
Is that your best lie?
When really you're regretting
I don't seem to get, or you seem to
forget
How you let this love die
And I don't really care that you're sad
You should've realized what you had
I only come around once
And you missed it standing right in
front
You could've had the world
But you couldn't handle this girl
All that I had to offer
You needed less
So you thought you'd find it in her

To have me you didn't deserve
And to do me dirty, you had nerve
I wasn't trying to change you
It was just your conscious coming
through
And now that you're all alone
It's haunting you that I'm gone too
And it's a little too late to negotiate
No, we can't work this out
There's nothing else left for us to talk
about

Miss Faithful

This is a story about little Miss Faithful
And for those of you who might be her
It can become quite tearful
As for her man
We'll just simply call him "Fuckboy"
I'll respect identity, revealing to none
But it won't change what he's done
It hurts to think and even write this
But it must be said
For me and the sake of all the good
girls
Whose hearts have been tread

So the story goes...

She stands alone
Beating at herself, she should've known
Sitting at the vanity staring into the
mirror, soliciting herself, sentiments
like a horror
What did she stay for?
Wondering why he doesn't care
anymore
Then thinking how maybe she herself
should have been unfaithful
With all that she gave
How could that man be so ungrateful?
He looked so bold and brave
He was her knight, her shining sir
But he played her for a fool
She thought he loved her

But apparently, she was just a tool
He does of another woman

The one that's not her
Whom she found
She had been sharing her world
An agreement in which was far from
mutual
And any excuse could never be suitable
Thinking that she was the only one
tenable
For a time, once in her life
A good man she thought she had won
Only to find that she was wrong
And had been living a lie all along

So in her regret...

She hates the fact that she cared so
much
Gave her heart, mind, and touch
Just to find out that she wasn't enough
Things still remain tough
She thought she was a good girl
Possessing all the right stuff
A strong, courageous, intelligent,
Loving woman, she was not belligerent
Forgiving, sweet and gentle,
Did nice things just because she was
humble
Supportive, full of laughter
Slow to anger,
Spontaneous, respectful, sexy,
beautiful

A soul most adventurous, but above all
faithful
Are these qualities undesirable and
hateful?

But then she thinks again...

She's a treasure that he's going to miss

That blind she was
And Him-unfaithful, undeserving,
Too busy in dirty fun
And to think that at one point
Lord have mercy, he was oh so sweet!
Then out of the blue
Took a turn down Loser Street
And now all he could seem to do
Was break her poor heart, shatter her
in two
And to think and sit to blame herself
She's not the reason he's into someone
else
And glad that she got some sense
But to convict herself, was the silliest
defense
Realizing she didn't deserve
To do such a thing, he had nerve

In conclusion to whom this poem has
applied...

There's more to it that makes this all
sad

It's that a faithful man
She and some of us have never had
Or one that didn't shoot us down
Condescend our character
Like being a good girl is an act of error
And it's not even that we try
But it's just who we are inside
And no one seems to appreciate
They think it's too good to be factual
To have something excellent
That never depreciates
So men will neglect
And go after the bullshit they're used to

The things that that the averages do
And can never get used to something
new
Things only possible to the dedicated
few
Not realizing that the answer is you
Not realizing that in an instant they
could stop
Stop looking, stop searching, and stop
flopping
And tune into you and witness
Experience the security of things
working
One day they'll all realize what they've
lost

Little Miss Faithful
To the men, I must ask
Was losing us worth the cost?

I Win

Hidden deep, so deep within
I hid my heart never to love again
Away from any and all men
Thinking to find me, nobody can
I'm the only one who knows who I am
They never did, I was just there to them
And from it all this poem stems
For the first time
I win

Heart Attack

Heart full of scars
Jabbed
Stabbed
Held hostage
Barred
Surprised
Disappointed in the road
But proud of me that I even got this far
Albeit with scars
Deteriorated heart muscle and what's
left of it
Somehow managed to pump through it
all
Too many times where I couldn't
breathe
But could only wheeze
Begging for them to stop killing me,
please

Cardiac arrest
World wars in my chest
Losing the battle in spite of giving my
best
It was tough coming above the rest
Guilty of loving both too hard and too
strong
And in the end, my love was somehow
peace be still
After all, they had done to kill

In a world not ready
The scale tips as too heavy
Trying to balance the fact
That some men truly aren't ready for
my heaven
For my world and space
I'm walking grace

Why am I always apologizing for my
Love and behavior?
Like Mr. Grey
Maybe I should arrange a lawyer
Have him draw me up a waiver
Stating to consent to the terms
Of being loved unconditionally
Where the rooms of pain in his soul
Are buried in the annuls of history

You would think by now I would be
wiser
After continuously getting the order
wrong
When they only put in for an appetizer
Having to plead to my manager (God) to
fix this explaining
"He didn't order the entrée."
Left to negotiate, removing my heart off
the tray
Where out of the paycheck of my soul I
pay
Knowing deep down, I'm not crazy,
Are they oblivious as to how we got
here?

To the things that they do and say?
Father forgive them
For they know not what they do
Oh shit, they knew

Forever am I saying sorry, I loved you
Maybe more than you wanted
Excuse me
I thought this is how it was supposed
to be
Me putting them first
Even when it hurts, fighting to the last
Always trying to tell me what I deserve
Gets on my absolute inner nerves

Instead of putting in the work
They divvy up excuses
Attempting to make me see them as
nothing
Telling me what they can't be
Trying to set me away from them
Free
Saying I deserve someone better or like
myself
Leaving me asking
Why can't he see the good that I see in
himself?
Never able to do the necessary for me
But swift to do much more to another
Until he is tired and wanders
Tries to come running back to me
Because it wasn't all it was cracked up
to be

Asserting to be ready for something
real,
Because he now sees that he once had
a deal
Beautiful reality dawns
Where they somehow thought I was
Waiting patiently for him, come on
A case of the exes
I don't play tic TAC toe
They must not have known

But really
What I want is...

Somebody to give it to me straight
Without all the curves,
A woman is supposed to be good
God is good to us, and that's whom I
serve
I'm tired of hearing that I'm too good
Too good of a woman for them

How about this...
God is too good for the both of us
But how come he still wants us?
Why do we want him?
Only a fool would settle for less and be
content enough to decline their
blessings without consent
I am a queen, sleep on me if you'd like
But I promise
I'll be your biggest weapon in case of a
strike

I'm not perfect
But wisdom never fails to prevail
On things that are correct, even when
they fail
Plenty of women out here
But beware of their deposits
everywhere
What can you really do with a bounced
check?

Am I not human?
I'm done trying to prove it
Unfortunately
Our culture for love has been ruined
I no longer know what I'm doing
Or where this is going
Lovesick
A nation with an infected generation
like a congenital bug
Love was never meant to be a hard tag
Nor was it meant to be easy
But how to love anymore makes me
uneasy
Soulmates to fuckmates
Queens to pawns
I'm out of moves
Love, for you
I have nothing but shrugs

Genuine

I guess it's in my blood
The way that I love like a raging flood
How deeply I feel
At the hard degree that I come
Every bit of it real
And when you have it your hands
Don't be a fool and let it drain like sand
Because guaranteed, finally
It'll be the best love you'll ever know
The best aside from God and family
The best you can ever show
The best you can ever seek to find in a
soul
A soul mate without foul

Hard to digest, hard to face
But I will absorb and compact your
mess
Take a seat and let me do the rest
And make a home in my chest

I like to think I end searching
And just when I think it's working
The system goes down
And we go rounds, in bounds
And split
Then they return saying
"I'm ready now."
I can't be that damn bad
If all I have crossed
Have tried to run back

As people say
I am real as it gets
Genuine
I am the shit

Finale

I will never write him another poem
I'm done after this one
I've moved on
And
All the positive feelings I used to
enclose for Him
Are at the moment gone
For a fraction of a moment, he left me
in ruins
Fools, I've learned
Have no idea what they are doing
Everything good I encapsulated
He used and abused
Somewhere he became confused
That I had zero power to leave him
He was wrong
Deluded imaginations recused

When a queen is misused
It's never that she doesn't know how to
refuse
It's that she believes and stands by her
Kingdom
Seeking his freedom
But when he threaten hers
Sentencing her
To the walls of his prison
To where she is unjustly asking for
forgiveness
That's when the chalice is poisoned
The energies rise high

And opens her eyes
Wider
To see that she cannot raise a man
Only his God can

About The Author

M.N. Bonds, is a 2014 graduate of North Carolina State University, veteran poetess, hopeless (sometimes hopeful) romantic, and free spirit.

M.N. Bonds may have grown up in the heart of dysfunction and had her share of challenging relationships well into early adulthood, but poetry served as her personal catalyst and healer. Through the power of her pen, she persevered past the darkness, and through it, strives to help others through their difficult times.

Today, M. N. Bonds writes about the triumphs and trials we all face in this life, as well as our divine light within, that when harnessed, serves as a lighthouse for other lost souls. Not just limiting herself to alliterative lines, she aspires to craft children's picture books in the near future.

Coming May 2018!
Aortic Chaos:
Fairytales of the Hopeless Romantic

CPSIA information can be obtained
at www.ICGtesting.com
Printed in the USA
BVHW051239300520
580415BV00006B/319